The Lost Boy

by
Mir Tamim Ansary

Upper Saddle River, New Jersey
www.globefearon.com

Project Editor: Brian Hawkes
Editorial Assistants: Jennifer Keezer, Jenna Thorsland
Art Supervision: Sharon Ferguson
Production Editor: Regina McAloney
Electronic Page Production: José López
Manufacturing Supervisor: Mark Cirillo
Cover Design: Sharon Ferguson
Illustrator: Jim McGinness

Copyright © 2000 by Globe Fearon, Inc., One Lake Street, Upper Saddle River, New Jersey, 07458, www.globefearon.com. All rights reserved. No part of this book may be reproduced or transmitted in any form or by any means, electronic or mechanical, including photocopying, recording, or by any information storage and retrieval system, without permission in writing from the publisher.

Printed in the United States of America
3 4 5 6 7 8 9 10 04 03 02 01 00

ISBN 0-130-23289-0

Contents

1. A Star Is Born 5

2. New Friends 12

3. A Day with Venus 18

4. The Lost Boy 27

5. Tyrone Comes Back 37

6. Questions Without Answers 42

7. Not Good Enough 50

8. In the Open 56

9. The Has-Been 67

10. Body Not Found 75

11. The Big Game 82

12. The Whole Story 90

1. A Star Is Born

"Stop them!"

The crowd is screaming with excitement. This is not just any basketball game. This is the Cougars against the Sharks. But the game is not going well. The Cougars are behind—by ten points.

Spider can't do anything to help. He is sitting on the bench where he always sits. Out of 12 guys on the team, he is number 12. Two years ago, he wasn't even on the team. He was not very big back then. No one called him Spider. He was Tom to his friends and "Hey, you" to everyone else. In school, he did just well enough to get by. In his classes, he never talked much. He was OK at playground games, but not great. There was just nothing special about him.

Back then, the game he played most was baseball. His best friend, Mark, was pretty good at it. He played in the park and sometimes Tom went along. Mark always made sure Tom was picked for a team. Tom was not a bad player. He was fast. He could field pretty well. He just couldn't hit. Mark would tell him, "Hey, some guys have it, and some guys don't." Tom would laugh—he didn't mind the joke.

Tom had been living with his aunt and uncle ever since his parents died. Uncle Robert owned a car shop. He did body work on cars. He had two guys working for him. When Tom and Mark became 14, Uncle Robert put them both to work. At first, he just had them help the older guys. But as time went by, he gave them chances to learn the business. As they learned, he gave them more to do—and more money, too.

Then Tom started to grow—and grow. In one year, he went from 5'4" to 6'3". His arms and legs became so long, he could hardly tell what they were doing anymore. His legs were always getting caught in things. His feet were just too far away to know what his head wanted. His hands had minds of their own. He could hardly make it across a room without falling over.

One day in the park, someone said to him, "Hey, Spider! Throw me the ball." No one had called him **Spider** before that day. After that day, everyone called him Spider. A name like that can stick for life. Tom had been Spider ever since that day.

Toward the end of that year, Spider was big enough to be in the basketball games on the other side of the park. Now Mark came with him sometimes. Spider always made sure Mark was picked. Spider was not that good at the game himself at first. But he could fill a lot of space under the basket.

His friends said he should try out for the high school basketball team. JFK High School had one of the best teams in the city. They even went to the state championship once. They didn't win, but you can't have everything. That team is still famous around the school. A picture of that team is still hanging in the office. But the boys from that team were all men now. One of them now sold used cars in town. You could see his ads on late night TV. "Come on down!" he would scream. "Let Mad Mack fix you up!" Another one was in politics.

Spider made the team when he was 16. He was happy just to be put on the team. He never started a game. In fact, he hardly ever played in a real game that year. But he thought the practice games were fun.

Now, however, Spider is in his last year of high school. He is growing into his body. His arms and legs feel like his own. He knows he is playing much better on the playground. He's no longer happy just to sit on the bench. He wants to be in some real games. The trouble is he plays power forward, and the team already has a star power forward. Tyrone is his name. He has been starting for three years. People say he **owns** the team. They say he is going to make a big name for himself in college ball. His name is in the paper sometimes. The team even has a good player to back him up. When Tyrone needs a rest, this other guy goes in for a few minutes. Coach Pack never keeps Tyrone out for much longer than that. So Spider never has his turn on the floor.

Tonight will be different. Spider is excited. He knows he is going to be in the game tonight. The other forward is out sick. When Tyrone needs a break, the coach will have to put Spider in the game. Spider keeps a close eye on the game, trying to get a feel for it. He wants to be ready.

Tyrone runs past the bench. He has the ball. He looks across the court. Dan is open. But Tyrone does not pass to him. He wants the basket for himself. He moves down the court into the corner. He stands there, waiting for someone to set a pick for him. But as he slows down, so do the others.

"Don't just stand around!" Spider thinks. "Pass the ball! Make something happen!" But he doesn't say it out loud. Bench guys just don't talk to the star that way.

Suddenly Tyrone sees his chance. He runs quickly to his left, stops, and turns. No one stands between him and the basket. He takes off like a truck going down the freeway. Nothing can stop him now. He leaves the ground—

The center for the other team steps in his way. He plants both feet and waits, a mountain of a man. Tyrone tries to change direction, but he is too late. He and the center crash together. Tyrone lands on the side of his foot and goes down with a high scream.

The whole team jumps to its feet. The coach runs out. The building falls quiet. After a long time, Coach Pack helps Tyrone to his feet, and people start to clap. "He's going to be OK." But their voices die away as Tyrone makes his way off the court. He can hardly walk. Everyone can see that he's badly hurt. He won't play again tonight.

The coach looks to the bench. He has no choice. He points to Spider. "Hey, you. End of the bench there—yes. You. Go in for Tyrone."

Spider jumps up. At last! This is not how he wanted it to happen, but his time has come at last. Now he has to make the most of it. He is so excited that his head starts to swim.

But as soon as play starts, Spider becomes calm. He runs down the court and finds his place in the corner. The ball goes to the other side. Then it comes back out to Dan, the guard. Spider throws up his arm. Dan sees him. Spider cuts to the basket. Dan lets the ball fly. Then time seems to slow down. Spider takes two long steps and leaves the ground. High above the basket his hands close around the ball, and then he slams it down and through.

The crowd sounds like big waves hitting a beach. Out of the corner of his eye, Spider sees Coach Pack. The old man is standing there looking like his eyes might fall out of his head. He had no idea Spider could finish like that on a pass.

The rest of the game is hard to remember later. Spider only knows he plays better than he has ever played in his life. But suddenly the clock is down to eight seconds. The Cougars are still behind by one point. Spider can't let his team lose on such a night—he just can't. His hands shoot out—he steals the ball! He goes flying toward the other end of the floor. The Shark guarding him tries to hold him back. That puts Spider on the line for two free throws.

The crowd is loud now. Everyone is screaming. Spider takes a long, full breath. The whole game is in his hands. If he makes one free throw, he will even up the score. If he makes two, he will put his team ahead. He gets his feet set and takes his shot. The ball goes up and through the basket like water.

One more.

One more, and he will have won it.

The crowd is quiet now—like one big animal holding its breath. Spider can feel all the eyes on him. He gets set. He throws the ball up.

A MISS!

But the ball comes right back to Spider! Without a moment of thought, he throws it up. The buzzer sounds, but the ball has already gone up into the air. If it's good, it will count. Then it falls right through the basket for 2 more points.

2. New Friends

The game is over, and the Cougars have won. Suddenly people are running at Spider from every direction. They are all screaming and laughing. "What a game! Just great!" Dan, the guard, is hitting Spider on the back so hard it hurts. "That slam when you first came in! That steal at the end. Oh, Spider—you were great!"

Spider feels as if he is in a dream. The coach puts an arm around him and moves him away from the others. Coach Pack never cracks a smile. But the look on his wooden face tonight is closer to a smile than Spider has ever seen.

"You did well. What did you say your name was again?"

"Spider. They call me Spider, Coach."

"Well, Spider, you did well. Can you play like

that every night? The news on Tyrone is not happy. He hurt his foot pretty bad, and he's going to be out for a few weeks. You're going to have to fill in. Can we count on you?"

"I'll do my best, Coach."

In the next three weeks, the Cougars play four more games. Tyrone comes to the games in street clothes. He just wants to see how the team does without him. What he sees makes him mad. The Cougars win all four games—and Spider plays a big part in every win. In the stands, people start to ask where Spider has been all this time. Then some of them say that Spider now **owns this team**. Coach Pack even gives Spider a few friendly smiles. Then one night, someone in the stands holds up a sign that says, "Tyrone Who?"

When Tyrone sees the sign, his face goes dark. Spider knows how he must feel. Spider wants to say something to Tyrone. But when he looks for Tyrone after the game, he's gone.

Spider changes and goes out to the street. Mark is waiting for him. As the friends start home, Spider hears a girl. "Oh, Spider—"

He turns around and sees Venus Green running after him. She's a girl that every guy in the school would like to go out with. Spider has never said a word to her before. She has never said a word to him. Yet, here she is calling out his name.

She puts a hand on his arm as she comes up. "That was some game, Sport! You must feel great!"

Spider can't seem to get his mouth working right. "I just—you know—did my part."

"Save it for the papers, Sport. I of all people know what winning feels like. You and me, Spider—we're two of a kind." Venus smiles. "How come we never got to know each other very well?"

"I guess—it's just one of those things." Spider can feel his face getting hot.

"Do you ever go to Mom's Home Cooking—that place on 9th? We might run into each other over there some time."

"Sure," says Spider. "Maybe."

"We could talk and get to know each other," says Venus. "Make up for lost time." She starts to walk away, then stops. "Oh—if you ever need to call me? I'm in the book. Or my mom is, anyway, and she has my same name."

After she's gone, Mark says, "What was that all about? You never told me about Venus Green. I guess now that you're a star, she wants you to ask her out."

"Should I call her?" Spider asks.

"You should call her," says Mark.

"But I wouldn't know what to say."

"You'll think of something," says Mark.

But Spider doesn't have to call her. The next day, a big red car drives up to The Body Shop, where he and Mark are hard at work. The car has a raised back end and a big loud engine. The driver is a guy known as Red—so-called because of his red hair. Next to him is his girlfriend, Donna. Everyone in the school knows who Red and Donna are. Red comes from a family with money. He always drives a great car and wears fancy clothes. He always knows what's hot and what's not. Most guys want to be part of his circle. Most girls want to be his girlfriend. But Red has picked Donna.

Venus is in the car, too. She sticks her head out as the car pulls up. "Hey, Spiderman," she says. "What's happening?"

"Just working," he says. He looks at Red. "You need some work done on this machine?"

Red laughs. "Are you kidding? I can't let just anyone work on my car."

"Spider is not just anyone," says Mark.

"Who asked you?" Red asks as he gives Mark a cool look.

Mark forgets what he wanted to say. "I—"

But Venus cuts in. "That boy is right, Red. Spider is not just anyone."

"What brings you here if not the car?" says Spider.

"You!" says Venus. "We're going for a little drive. We want you to come along."

"Well—" Spider looks at Mark. Uncle Robert lets the boys keep their own hours—as long as they have their work done. But Spider has a car to work on right now, and he has hardly started.

On the other hand, the most cool kids in the school are here at his door, asking him to join them. Venus is looking at him with her pretty green eyes. How can he turn down this chance? He says, "Well, I guess I could do this work later."

"Great!" says Donna. "Jump in. We'll drive by the Fast Stop, pick up something to eat—"

Mark says to Spider in a low voice, "I think your uncle really wanted you to fix that red car today."

"Oh, leave him alone," laughs Venus. "Spider is mine today!" She gives him a big smile and opens the car door for him.

Mark cleans off his hands on an old cloth. "Well," he says, "I guess we could work on these cars later." He starts to follow Spider to the car. But Venus pulls the door shut to keep him out. Through the window, she tells him, "Sorry, guy. Only room for 1 more."

Red laughs as he takes off. Mark is left behind with his mouth open. He doesn't even have time to say anything. Spider feels bad. "Stop!" he wants to say. "Let me out!" He doesn't want to go anywhere with people who act like that to his best friend. But somehow, the words never make it to his mouth. It's too late anyway—isn't it? The harm is done. He can tell Mark how sorry he is later. For now, he had better not do anything to lose face with his new friends.

3. A Day with Venus

Spider and his new friends drive around for a long time. The others talk and laugh. Spider tries to forget about Mark, but it's hard. Red talks about cars and how he wants to be a race car driver. Already he has been in some races—and done well. He has even won some money. His dad is going to set him up with a race car of his own someday.

Donna talks about her hopes, too. She wants to act on TV. When she leaves high school, she will move to L.A. "I was there last summer," she tells Spider. "I know some people." She names the people. Spider has no idea who they are. But he knows they must be important from the way Donna says their names.

"Great," he says.

"Oh, yes," she goes on, "I have lots of telephone numbers to call when I get to L.A. People tell me I have what it takes to break into show business. I mean, how would I know? I just listen to what people tell me."

Venus laughs, "Well," she says, "I can't act like you, Donna, and I can't race cars like Red. I guess I will have to get by on my looks." She shows off her white teeth in a big smile. Venus wants to be a model—that's no secret. She has already done some ads for a big clothes store in town. Her picture has been in the newspaper.

Spider knows it is his turn now. He should talk about basketball. He should talk about some big name college that just won't leave him alone. He should talk about all the money he will make in the NBA. But this is all too new. No college has been after Spider. He has never thought about the NBA. As far as he knows, he will go to work in his uncle's shop full time after high school. This is not what the others want to hear. So he says nothing.

Around 3:00, Venus wants to go to the park. Red has somewhere else to be, so he lets Venus and Spider out at Page Street. Venus says, "There is a hot dog stand at the mouth of the park. Buy some dogs. I'll be over there. I'll find a place for us to sit that's out of the sun."

Spider goes to the stand. The girl working there is someone he has seen before. "Hey," he says, "don't you go to my school?"

She looks at him. "Maybe. Is your name Fly?"

"Spider," he tells her.

"Oh, yes," she says. "I remember it was some kind of insect. You were in my science class last year."

The girl is short and has long black hair. She looks OK, but there is nothing special about her. She will never make money as a model like Venus. Yet, Spider can't take his eyes off her. He doesn't know why, but he just wants to hang around the hot dog stand. Maybe it's the very fact that she **isn't** some kind of fancy star.

But why won't she look at him the way Venus does? Does she know who he is? Maybe she needs a little help. He says, "Did you catch the game last night?"

"What game?" she says.

"Basketball. The Cougars. I'm on the team, you know."

"Are you?" she says. "I never go to basketball games. Sorry." She turns to face a man who has just come up.

"Two dogs," says the man. Spider can feel the man crowd him to one side. Nothing like this would happen to him on a basketball court. He's not about to let it happen here. He has to push a little to hold his space. The man says, "Hey! What is your problem?"

"I didn't get your name," Spider says to the girl.

"Diana," she says. Then she smiles. "I don't think you should keep your girlfriend waiting."

"Oh?" Spider turns. Venus is waving at him.

"What's taking you so long?" she calls. "Come over here!"

"Well," says Spider to the girl behind the hot dog stand, "good to see you again." He makes his way over to Venus. Something must be wrong with him, he is thinking. Here he is with a girl who could be a famous model one day. Just about any guy in school would change places with him. Yet, all he wants is to go back and talk to that girl at the hot dog stand. Maybe being a star takes some getting used to. Venus is telling him about a problem she had with her hair the day she did an ad for the Mountain Shop. He can't keep his mind on her story. But he says, "Oh" and "Yes" from time to time, just to keep her happy.

"I don't think you should keep your girlfriend waiting."

Then suddenly he sees something moving. He looks around. A boy has come up behind them. He's about to take their bag of food.

"Just what do you think you're doing?" Spider asks him.

The kid jumps for the bag and takes off with it.

"Hey!" Spider cries.

"What?" Venus looks around. "Why, that dirty little kid!"

"Come back here, you!" Spider goes running after the boy.

The kid turns. Spider sees his face for a moment. That face burns a picture into Spider's mind. The kid looked scared. He looked sad. No—it was more than that. He looked like a hurt animal running for his life.

Spider keeps after him, sure that he can catch up. But he finds out that bigger is not always better. The kid comes to a high wall. The kid gets down and pushes his way through a hole under the wall. Spider is too late to catch the kid. Spider is too big to go through the hole. He tries to go over the wall. It's too high. He runs around it just in time to see the kid race across the street and over a mountain of boxes behind a shop. Spider tries to follow the kid over the boxes, but they give way under him. He falls back to the ground.

He picks himself up, feeling mad and dirty. The kid is gone. He must have gotten into the building somehow. Spider doesn't know why he should feel so strongly about it. So the kid ran away with his hot dog—so what? He can always buy another one. Then it hits him that he isn't mad, really. He's sad more than anything.

He stops at the hot dog stand on the way back. "Did you see that kid?" he asks Diana.

"What kid?" she says.

"Some little kid took off with our hot dogs. Can you beat it? He got away with our drinks, too."

"I'm sorry," says Diana. He can tell what she is thinking. "Why tell me?"

Spider goes back to Venus, who says, "Oh no! Don't tell me you let that kid get away!"

"Yes, he got away." Spider sits down. "Where do you think he came from, Venus? He looked so scared! Do you think he's homeless, living in the park? No! A boy that young! He couldn't be, could he?"

Venus shakes her head. "I don't know. Who cares? He was a dirty little thief. All we can do is call the cops, I guess."

"The cops?" Spider studies her closely. "What are they going to do? The kid is long gone."

"Maybe he has a hiding place around here," says Venus. "The cops can catch him. That's what they're good at."

"Catch him and then what?" says Spider.

"I don't know. Look, it's not our problem, OK?" She gives him a shake. "This is our time to be together. Don't ruin it. I want us to have a good time."

"But that kid must be in trouble. We can't just turn our back on him," says Spider. "That's not my idea of a good time."

"Well," says Venus. "I guess you have to make up your mind, don't you? Do you want us to get to know each other better? Or do you want to do social work?"

Spider just looks at her. After awhile she turns away. "You're no fun at all," she says.

They finish their food without much more talk. Then Spider takes Venus home. After that, he goes to a movie by himself. He knows that he has made a choice of some kind. He just doesn't know what it is.

4. The Lost Boy

When Spider comes home, his uncle meets him at the door. "Where have you been, Tom?"

"Out with some friends," says Spider. "Why?"

"I guess you're a star now. You can do whatever you want," says his uncle. "Is that it? Now that you're a star, let good old Mark finish the work?"

"I never said Mark should do my work, Uncle Robert. I—"

"Did you, or did you not say you were going to work on that red car today?" his uncle says.

"I did! I'm going to get to it right now." Spider starts to walk past his uncle.

But his uncle says, "Not so fast. You said you were going to fix it today—not tonight!"

"What?" Spider stops and turns.

"Tonight is not good enough! You gave me your word you would have it done today!"

"But isn't tonight just as good?" says Spider. "The guy isn't going to pick up the car till tomorrow, is he?"

"That's not the point!" his uncle cries. The point is **you gave me your word**. That has to mean something! If you say **today**, it has to be today! Or else, pretty soon, your word won't be worth anything. Your word is all you have in the end. That's all a man really has, Tom!"

"I didn't think it was important if it was today or tonight, Uncle. I still don't. I'll fix the car by tomorrow. That's what I should have said, if I didn't. I'll stay up all night if I have to. You have my word on **that**."

"I guess that will have to do." The old man still doesn't look happy.

Spider keeps his word, but he has to stay up late to do it. He gets to school on time the next day, but he can't keep his eyes open in science class. Later he meets Mark and tells him how sorry he is about yesterday. Mark wants to hear all about Venus. Spider goes on to tell him about the little kid in the park. Mark listens, but he doesn't know why Spider has such strong feelings about it. "It's not your problem, is it?" he asks.

Spider makes it to basketball practice a few minutes late. He feels slow that day. Coach Pack pulls him out. "What's wrong?"

"Nothing. I was working late," Spider tells him.

"Well," says the coach, "if you have any problems, you come talk to me. You're our main man now. You can't just be thinking of yourself anymore. You have to think about the team."

"Sure, Coach." But Spider is not thinking about himself, or the team. He is thinking about that kid in the park.

After practice, Spider drives to the park. He looks all over for the kid, but sees no sign of him. The next day he goes to the park before practice. This time he has a new idea. He buys hot dogs and drinks from Diana, who is at the stand again.

She says, "Where is your girlfriend today?"

"She isn't my girlfriend," says Spider. "I like you better."

"Cut it out," says Diana. "I don't go out with sports guys. They're too full of themselves." She gives him his change. "You're going to eat all that by yourself?"

"No. There's a homeless kid somewhere in this park. I'm going to try and find him."

"Oh?" She looks at Spider as if she has just seen him for the first time.

Spider goes to the corner where he and Venus had been sitting. He has that corner to himself today. He puts the bag down and sits with his back to it. He has a little piece of glass in his pocket. He takes it out and sets it against his foot. In the glass, he can see the bag behind him and the green wall of plants behind that. Spider sits very still and just waits.

Suddenly it happens. The boy sticks his small dirty face out of the wall of plants. He must have been hiding in there all along. He takes a quick look right and left. Then, carefully, he steps out into the open. He looks at Spider's back for a moment and then takes another careful step closer. His eyes stay on that bag of food.

Spider moves a little. It isn't much, but it makes the kid freeze. Spider knows he must not move again. After a long time, the kids starts toward the bag again. Soon he is so close that Spider can hear his breath.

The boy sticks his small dirty face out of the wall of plants.

In a low voice, Spider says, "Want something to eat? I have enough—"

The kid makes no sound.

"Are you there?" Spider asks.

Time passes.

"Can you talk?" Spider asks.

More time passes. Then Spider hears one quiet word from a very small voice: "Yes."

"Good." Still Spider does not move. "I know you're scared… But don't be scared of me. I would never hurt you. I won't even try to catch you. OK? You have my word." He waits a moment for an answer. When he doesn't hear one, he keeps talking. "OK, good. We understand each other. I'm going to turn around now. Don't be scared. I won't get up. If you want to run away, go right ahead. I won't come after you. Understand all that?"

Again that very small voice says, "Yes."

Spider turns around. The kid is standing a few feet away. He is wearing jeans and a yellow top. He looks about five years old. His face is very dirty. Spider can see that he has a bad cold.

"Hi." Spider smiles at the boy.

The boy moves his mouth. It looks like he might have said, "Hi," but the word doesn't come out. He looks at the bag.

"You could use some food, I guess." Spider takes a hot dog out for himself and pushes the bag forward. Then he moves back. He knows he has to give the little boy a lot of space. It is the only way he will feel safe. When Spider is far enough away, the boy takes the bag. He opens it, pulls out some food, and starts to eat as fast as he can. But his eyes are like those of a little animal. They never stop looking here and looking there.

Spider just eats his own hot dog. He tries to act as if he is not even interested in the boy. After awhile, the kid sits down and looks in the bag again.

"My name is Tom," says Spider. "Most people call me Spider. What is your name?"

"I don't know," says the boy.

"You don't know?" Spider turns this answer over in his mind. The boy is young, but not that young. How could he not know his own name? "You live around here?"

The boy points to the wall of plants.

"You live in there?" says Spider.

But the boy shakes his head. Spider takes a guess at what he means. "You live somewhere else? Where is your house?"

"I don't know," says the boy. He comes closer to Spider.

"You have family around here?"

At this question, the boy's eyes start to water. "I don't know," he says. Then he starts to cry.

Spider doesn't know what to do. "There, there," he says. But the words don't seem to help much. The boy keeps crying. In fact, he puts his face down against his hands and cries even harder. "That's OK," says Spider. "Go ahead and cry. Nothing wrong with crying."

So the boy keeps crying till he cries himself out. Then at last he stops shaking. He looks up at Spider and says, "I'm scared."

"Well, who wouldn't be?" says Spider. "You've been alone. But now I'm here to help you. Don't be scared anymore, OK?"

"OK," says the boy.

"Listen, I'm going for help," says Spider. "You stay here. I'll be right back."

"No!" The boy's eyes fill up with that same look again: sad and scared and lost. "Don't leave me here!"

"Come with me then. We'll go together."

The boy does not ask where they are going. He just takes Spider's hand and walks along next to him. Spider feels like a big brother. It is a good feeling.

Spider takes the little guy to the hot dog stand. "This is my good friend, Diana," he says. "Will you stay with her a minute till I make a telephone call?"

Diana says, "Is this—?"

"Yes," says Spider. He doesn't want her to say anything that might make the boy sad again.

The boy studies Diana with his big, dark eyes. "You're not my mom," he says at last.

"No, but she's your friend," says Spider. "That's a good thing, too."

"OK." The boy makes up his mind: he likes Diana, too.

Spider calls the police and tells them about the boy. The police come in less than 15 minutes. They bring along a social worker named Jean

Strauss. She smiles at Spider and says, "We'll take over now. You've done very well."

But the little boy looks scared again. "Where are they taking me?" he cries, as Mrs. Strauss moves him toward her car. "Spider! Help!"

Spider goes to the boy quickly. "These are good people, too. They'll buy some food for you, clean you up. Take care of that cold. I have to go now, but I'll see you soon." He looks up at the social worker. "Right? Can I do that?"

"I don't see why not," she says. "Give me your number. I'll let you know what is happening."

As they walk away, Spider hears the boy telling Mrs. Strauss: "He's not my brother. But he's my friend. Friends are good, too."

5. Tyrone Comes Back

Spider gets to practice a few minutes late. The team is standing around in a circle. Coach Pack waves him over to join the group. As soon as Spider takes his place in the circle, he sees Tyrone standing across from him. Everyone is quiet.

Coach Pack says, "Men. You all know Tyrone was our starting power forward before he was hurt. Now he's back."

One of the players says, "You ready to play again, Tyrone?"

Coach Pack gives the answer. "Both Tyrone and the doctor say 'Yes.' Which brings us to a question. Spider has done a great job these past few weeks. Any other year, any other team, he would be starting."

Spider feels sad, but he has seen this coming. He's ready for it. Little Dan says, "Spider is going back to the bench? You can't do that!"

"Hey!" The coach turns on Dan. "I say who starts and who doesn't. I'm the coach. Got that? Good. Second of all, you don't know what I'm going to do. Listen up, and let me tell you. Don't put words in my mouth."

"Sorry," says Dan.

The coach looks down at the ground for a moment. Then he looks up again. "I have a rule. No one loses his job on this team because he is hurt. I pull guys out only because they're not doing the job. Tyrone was doing the job." The coach looks around.

"But then I have this other rule," he goes on. "I always tell my guys every year is a whole new page. At the start of the year, every guy has the same shot. Don't tell me what you did last year. Prove it to me this year. That's what I always say. But this year, I didn't follow my own rule. I know it now because I see the way Spider has been playing. I never gave him a real look at the start of the year. Tyrone has always been so good. It made me close my eyes. Tyrone had the lock on the job. Spider never had a real shot at it."

"You mean you're going to bench Tyrone?" cries Mack, the team center. He and Tyrone are best friends. "You can't do that, Coach!"

Dan cries out, "But Spider is better. Why don't you think of the team for once, Mack!"

Suddenly everyone is screaming. Coach Pack cuts them short.

"Stop it! Don't you guys listen? What did I just tell Dan? I'm the coach. Don't put words in my mouth. You don't know what I'm going to do. Listen up. Did I say I was going to bench Tyrone?"

"No."

"What did I say I was going to do?"

"I don't know. I guess you didn't say."

"That's right. I didn't say." The coach looks around from face to face. Suddenly Spider can tell he doesn't know what to do. Coach Pack is between a rock and a hard place. He has to keep his team together. But whatever he does will make some guys on the team mad.

"Well, Coach," Dan says at last. "What's it going to be?"

Right then the coach makes up his mind. "I'm going to play you both."

"Both? But one of them will have to start!" cries Dan.

"One will start, one will close. You'll both get minutes. **BUT!**" The coach raises one hand to stop anyone else from talking. "Only for a few weeks. Till one of you can prove himself."

He gives the team time to think about this. Spider looks at Tyrone. Tyrone looks back at him with hard, cool eyes.

The coach goes on. "I might as well tell you right now. I don't think either of you is going to win this thing on skills. Go ahead and prove me wrong, but I don't think you can. Because when it comes to skills, I think you 2 are even. But great basketball isn't just about skills."

"No," says Dan. "You have to be quick, too."

"That's not what I had in mind," says Coach Pack. "I want you men to understand something bigger. A great player works hard, gives 100% to his game, sets an example—and something more. He brings his team together. If one of you 2 men can show me this something more, he's going to start. So if you come to practice late, you lose points. I don't care how well you play. If you bad mouth other guys on your team, I don't care about your skills. Am I getting through to you?"

"I think we get it, Coach," says Tyrone.

"Good. Then go play some ball," says Coach Pack.

6. Questions Without Answers

The next day Spider gets a telephone call. "Mr. Spider?"

"Just Spider will do. Who is this?" Spider asks.

"Matthew Peary with Missing Persons. We have some questions about Little Bill—the boy you found in the park."

"You know his name already? Great!" says Spider.

"No," says the cop. "Bill is just a name we picked out of a hat. We had to call him something, and Bill is better than a number. We would like to talk to you in person. Could you come in around 3:00 today?"

"Sure," says Spider. So later that day, he goes to see Peary in his office. Two other people are there: Mrs. Strauss, the social worker; and Jared Teller, a doctor.

Peary asks Spider a lot of questions about the little boy. He wants details. Spider tells him all he can. At last the cop shakes his head. "It just doesn't add up," he says.

"How so?" Spider asks.

"Well," says Peary, "think about it. This kid turns up in the park. His clothes are dirty—but they're pretty new. He has a bad cold, but his bones don't show. He has enough to eat. In fact, from everything we can see, this little boy had a good home till a few days ago. There must be someone in the world who cares about him. Yet, no one is looking for him. If his family had gone to the police, Missing Persons would have some paperwork on him. His family would have had to fill out some forms. The information would be in our computer. His picture would be there for us to pull up. But we've got nothing. We looked at every piece of news on every kid missing in the last month. There was no one who sounds or looks like this little boy."

"Maybe he comes from another city," says Spider.

"The computer picks up information from the whole state."

"Maybe his family doesn't know he's gone?"

"That's not an answer. It's another question. How could no one know the kid is gone? What kind of family could he have?"

"I see what you mean," says Spider.

"You found the kid yesterday," says Peary. "You saw him in the park 2 days before that. So right there, he's been gone from home 3 days. He might have been sleeping in the park 1 or 2 days already, from what you say. Yet, no one knows he's gone? Give me a break!"

"How is he holding up?" Spider asks. "Where is he now?"

Mrs. Strauss says, "We've put him in a good foster home now. We work with these parents a lot. But they have 2 kids of their own. They are already taking care of 2 other foster kids. So the boy is safe, but no one has much time for him.

Now the doctor cuts in. "If I may?"

"Go ahead," says Mrs. Strauss.

"I've looked the boy over," the doctor tells Spider. "I've run some tests. Other than the cold, there is nothing wrong with him. But he has this mark on his head. He must have been hit there—

some kind of accident, I would guess. That must have been how he lost his memory. Now if a doctor had seen him right away, things might have been different. But that's just when he got lost, it looks like. So when he came to, he found himself alone, cold, scared, and lost."

"The point is—" says Mrs. Strauss.

But the doctor cuts in. "If I may finish? Yes. The point is, when a thing like this happens, the memory often comes back. But it may take a little push. The boy needs to see things that he knows—people, places. The trouble is we don't know where he comes from. He may live on the other side of town for all we know. Someone has to drive him around from neighborhood to neighborhood. It's going to take a lot of time."

"His foster parents don't have that kind of time, you see," Mrs. Strauss cuts in.

"The police—" says Peary. "Well, you know how it is."

All of them end up just looking at Spider.

"You want me to do it?" says Spider. "I'll be happy to."

"One more thing," says Peary. "Talk to the boy as you drive him around. He may open up to you more than anyone else. See if you can get any more information out of him. Because so far we have nothing to go on."

The next day, Spider goes to see Little Bill. The boy's foster mom is happy to see Spider. "He was asking for you all of yesterday. Today he suddenly started screaming in his sleep. I just don't know what to do with this one. He's a problem."

Spider sits down with Bill. "Did you have a bad dream?"

"I saw something, Spider. I was real scared."

"We all have them, kid. What did you see—a monster?"

"Cars," says the boy. "I saw lots of cars. They were all moving. But they were empty."

"It was just a bad dream," says Spider.

"It wasn't a dream," says the boy. "I remember I was in one of those cars. No one was driving. All the cars were moving by themselves. I remember now. They were new. They were empty, and I was the only one in them. I couldn't make them stop. I couldn't get out. I remember! It really happened! Really!" His voice keeps going up as he talks.

The foster mom points to her own head as if to say, "He's out of his mind." Out loud she says, "It was just a dream, Bill. **JUST A BAD DREAM—OK?**"

"No! It wasn't!" cries Bill.

Spider raises his hand to quiet the boy. He gives the foster mom a **go away** look. "I believe you, Bill," he says. "But tell me more. Do you remember how you got out of the car?"

"I don't know," says Bill. Then, "Yes, I do." He thinks for a moment. "I remember falling out," he says at last.

"Out of a moving car?" Spider says.

"No. I was trying to get out, and then there was this man—"

"What man?"

"The big man!" says Bill. "He was just there! He screamed and made me fall. That man! I was scared. He was a big man."

Spider asks, "Is that when you hurt your head?" Falling out of a moving car would do it, he thinks.

"No," says Bill. "My head hurt already. But the man screamed, and I was scared. He called me names and tried to catch me."

"Do you remember anything about the man?"

"Like what?" says the boy.

"Well, for example, what was he wearing?"

"Clothes!" says the little boy right away.

"I mean, what kind of clothes?"

"Driving clothes. He was the driver," says Bill.

"I thought you said there was no driver," says Spider.

"Oh, yes." Now the little boy isn't sure. "Well, maybe they weren't driving clothes. But anyway, they were green."

The foster mom lets out a low laugh. "Now do you see what I have to go through?" she says.

Spider says, "Listen, Bill, I have to go now. But tomorrow—"

"Where are you going?" says the boy.

"To basketball practice. But tomorrow—"

"You play basketball? Are you a star?" Bill wants to know.

"Well, in a small way, I guess—but not for long, if I miss practice. I'll take you out for a drive tomorrow. We'll have a good time. OK, Bill?"

The kid looks sad. "You're not going to come back," he says.

"Of course, I will," says Spider. "I give you my word. OK?"

"OK," the little boy says, as he lets go of Spider's hand. He seems to feel that Spider's word is good.

7. Not Good Enough

Bill seems to feel better the next day. His cold is going away. "Where are we going?" he asks, when they are in the car.

"We're just going to drive around for awhile. I want you to look for anything you've seen before. Houses, streets, people—anything. Let's start at the north end of town. What do you say? Park Woods. Maybe you're a rich kid."

"If I'm rich, you'll get money."

Spider laughs. "Don't even think that way, kid. I'm helping you just because I like you. Understand?"

Bill starts out very excited. He's sure he will find his home. But he doesn't see anything he remembers all day. After 2 hours, Spider says, "Well, that's just about every street in Park Woods. Tomorrow we'll try Gold Beach."

Then on the way back, Bill cries, "There's a place I know."

"That's the park," says Spider. "That doesn't count. That's where we found you."

"Yes, but my friend lives there."

"What friend?"

"The woman you like."

"Venus?" Spider laughs.

"Not her. The one you like. She lives in the park," says Bill. "She gives people hot dogs."

"Oh—Diana! She doesn't live in the park. She just works there," says Spider. "Sure. Let's stop and see her. Good idea."

"She gave me a hot dog," says Bill.

Spider takes Bill to the stand where Diana is working. When Bill goes running off playing some little game, Spider has a chance to talk to Diana. He tells her all about the boy.

"Poor little guy," she says. "Maybe I could take him around some days, too."

"That would be good. I'll take you to meet his foster parents. You should meet his social worker, too."

Just then Bill comes running up. He looks up at Diana for awhile. "You're pretty," he says. He turns to Spider. "Don't you think so?"

"Yes, I do. Very pretty."

"Cut it out," says Diana. "You don't have to say that."

"Spider likes you," says the boy. "He plays basketball. He's a star. But not for long if he doesn't practice. Will you take me to see him play?"

Diana laughs. "Sorry, kid. I don't go to sports events. But maybe I can take you to a movie sometime."

"Right now!" cries the little boy. "We can all go. You can be the mom, and Spider can be my dad."

Just then Spider happens to look at his watch. "Oh, no! I'm late for practice. Come on, Bill. I have to take you back to the foster home."

"No," cries Bill. "I want to see a movie."

"Sorry, Bill. Another day." Spider takes the boy by the hand and pulls him toward the car. Diana shakes her head. She must think he's being mean to the kid. Spider wants to tell her why getting to practice is so important. But there is too much to say and not enough time. He has no choice, but to let it go. But he ends up feeling low and mean. "I've let them both down," he thinks.

He is late for practice. Again. Tyrone is already there, shooting free throws. Spider can't keep his mind on basketball that day. He keeps hearing Little Bill in his mind. Then he's mad at himself and puts everything he has into his game. He makes 3 baskets in 32 seconds. He steals the ball 2 times. He blocks a shot.

But the coach is not happy with him. "Too much up and down," he says. Some of the guys on the team are not happy, either. Spider feels that he has let them all down. When practice is over, he can't meet their eyes. He changes clothes and starts for home. Mark is not waiting for him on the street. Spider has not seen much of Mark for awhile. He goes home alone.

The front room of the house is dark. His aunt and uncle are in the back. "You're late," says his uncle. "Again."

"I'm sorry," says Spider. "Practice went a little long today."

"Oh, well. Practice is the most important thing, I guess. Isn't it? You said you would work on that green car yesterday. But you didn't do it."

"I know. I'm sorry. I had to take Little Bill around town—"

"Don't bring Little Bill into this. He's not taking up your time. It's basketball. You think the whole world goes around you now that you're a star. Getting your hands dirty, working on cars—you're above that now. Old Uncle Robert and his shop aren't worth your time."

"That's not fair!" Spider cries out. "I never said things like that. I don't act that way!" He feels as if he is about to fall over—and he still has homework to do.

"You listen to your uncle," says his aunt. "He knows what he's talking about."

"Tom, didn't we talk about how important it is to keep your word?" his uncle says. "Didn't we, Tom?"

"I didn't give you my word that the green car would be done tonight, Uncle Robert. I said I would do my best. I'm doing my best."

"Well, your best is not good enough. Spider, when your parents passed away, your aunt and I took you in. No questions asked. I told your aunt that as soon as you were old enough, I would make a place for you in my shop. I told your aunt

I'm going to give that boy a start in life. Now you're almost out of high school, Tom. You have to start thinking about your real life. What are you going to do with it? I'm trying my best to help you. But you have to do your part, too. Day after day, I find out you haven't done your work. Don't tell me this is about helping some little kid. You're out running around with all your hot new friends. All of a sudden, you're a big man around town. Well, I told you before. I'm going to tell you again—one last time. You have to make some choices. You can't have your head in the stars and your feet on the ground at the same time. It has to be one or the other. I tell you, Tom, if you weren't family, I would have let you go. No one said to stop playing basketball. Go ahead and play in the park. Have your fun. You're young. But basketball is not your life. It's just a game. The minute it starts to cut into your real life, you have to let it go. You just have to. Can you play on this team without letting it take over your life? Make a choice, Tom."

8. In the Open

After that, Spider does his best to catch up. He tries to give 100% to Bill. But he never has as much time as the little boy needs. He tries to get ahead of his work at the shop. But there is always too much of it. He tries to give 100% to the team. But he keeps getting to practice late.

At this time of year, all the games are important. But one game stands above the others like a mountain. This is the game against the Sharks, a team from another city. The Cougars and the Sharks play each other two times a year. The Cougars won the first game this year. Whoever wins the second one will go on to play for the state championship. This is the biggest game of the year.

One day, a week before this big game, Spider is late to practice again. The coach is mad. After practice, he calls Spider into his office.

"Yes, Coach?"

"Sit down," says Coach Pack.

Spider sits.

The coach looks him in the eye. "I don't know an easy way to say this."

He's made up his mind, Spider thinks. I'm going back to the bench. He feels cold inside. "Just say it, Coach. I can take it."

"Spider, I just want to know what's going on with you. Time and again, you come to practice late. Some days you look like you didn't sleep all night. You have a big, dark circle under each eye. Sometimes—"

"Coach," Spider cuts in.

"Yes? What have you got to say for yourself? I want to hear it."

"Basketball means a lot to me, but I have other things on my mind. I'm trying to keep up in my classes. I'm trying to hold down a job after school, and other things."

"What things? That's what I want to hear about. You can't live the fast life and be on the team, too. You can't stay out till all hours with your friends and still—"

"I don't do that, Coach. It's not like you think. I haven't told anyone on the team yet. I guess other guys wouldn't understand. They would laugh at me."

"Yes? But what? Tell me," says the coach.

"Well, OK. I was in the park one day, and I found a lost boy."

"A lost boy!"

"Yes. He was living in the park." Then Spider goes on to tell Coach Pack the whole sad story. "Ever since then, I've been looking after the little guy," he says. "I just try to be there for him, because no one else really seems to care. I mean, the cops are trying. This foster family does its best. But he needs more. I just try to be that something more. Maybe it's one too many things, but what am I supposed to do?"

The coach sits for a long time, looking at him. At last he says, "I hope you are not giving me a line, Spider."

"No, Coach. But if you don't believe me, I don't know what more to say. Call Matthew Peary at Missing Persons, I guess. That would be the only other thing."

"What about these other stories going around about you?"

"What stories?"

"That you're doing a drug of some kind," says the coach.

"What?" Spider feels like someone has hit him in the face with a block of ice. "Who says that?"

"Well, who says it is not important," says the coach. "The point is—"

"Not important!" Spider jumps to his feet. "Sorry, Coach. Not to you, maybe. But to me, it's everything. Who would tell a dirty story like that about me? Coach, I want to know!"

"I don't want to name names here," says the coach. "The point—"

"What about my name?" Spider cries out. "Someone named my name! Don't I have a right to know who? Don't I have a right to face the guy?"

Suddenly the coach goes red in the face. "I gave my word I wouldn't tell."

"Oh? Well, I guess I have to go out there and talk to the guys myself."

Spider starts out of the office. Coach Pack calls

out, "Spider! Come back! I'm not done."

Spider turns. "Something else, Coach?"

"I just wanted to say—wait up. I'll come with you."

They go out to the floor. The whole team is still out there. Coach Pack says, "Listen up, men. We have some trouble on this team, and we're going to air it out right here and now. Spider has something to say. Then I'm going to say a few words. Go ahead, Spider."

So Spider starts into it. He says, "Guys. You all know I haven't been giving this team 100%. Now I want to tell you why. I suppose you could say I've had a lot on my mind and let it go at that. But I think I've got to put it right on the table. The fact is, it comes down to one choice. I've got this little kid I take care of."

Mack breaks into a smile. Someone laughs. Someone else says, "A little kid?"

"This has been taking a lot out of me. Time, for one thing, but it's more than time. This kid is lost. He has no family. No family—you guys know what that feels like? What it means? He has no memory. He doesn't even know his name. I found him, and I gave him my word that I would stick by him till he was back home. He's only five or six years old. Some of you may not know this, but I lost my own parents when I was seven. I've been living with my aunt and uncle ever since. They're great, they're like parents to me. But I guess way inside somewhere I've always had this feeling I'm a lost kid myself. So I know how this little boy feels—alone in the world—not even knowing who he is… There are times when he's needed more than I can give. I thought I'd walk away from this. You can't really help this kid. Just go play ball, do something you can really do. Then I would look at that kid, and I couldn't turn my back on him. So I have been doing the best I can for him and for the team. Maybe I have not had 100% to give here. You know what I can do with 90%. You guys have to say if it's enough."

At first when Spider stops talking, no one says a word.

Then Tyrone says, "I didn't know any of this. I was wrong about you." He looks quickly around at the others.

Coach Pack says, "My turn."

Tyrone is scared. The coach says, "One of you men came to me a few days ago and said you had a secret about another player on the team. You asked me not to tell anyone where it came from. I gave you my word. I'm sorry now that I did, but what's done is done. I will stick to my word. But I think you should stand up now—you know who you are. Tell everyone what you told me. Let's put this whole thing in the open."

Each guy on the team looks at the other. At last, Tyrone says, "It was me. I went to Coach and told him that maybe Spider was doing some kind of drug."

"What?" screams Dan.

"That's what I thought," Tyrone cries out. "How was I supposed to know? He comes in late all the time. You can tell he needs sleep. I've seen all those signs before!"

"So you just took a guess?" Dan steps toward Tyrone. He's ready to hit the big guy.

Spider holds him back. "Dan, let's not fight about this." Then he looks Tyrone in the eye. "Let me say this out loud. I do not take any kind of drug!"

"I know—I know. I believe you," Tyrone says quickly, under his breath."

"So you just took a guess?" Dan steps toward Tyrone. He's ready to hit the big guy.

Coach says, "Anything else, Tyrone?"

"I'm sorry." Tyrone looks up now. "I was way out of line talking like that. It won't happen again."

"Talk like that can ruin a man," says Coach.

The whole team is looking at Tyrone. Not one face looks friendly.

Spider says, "All right. You said you're sorry. You said it won't happen again. That's the end of it. Let's you and me shake hands now, Tyrone. Let's be on the same team again."

Tyrone, still hanging his head, takes Spider's hand.

Then the whole team starts to clap.

Spider breaks into a smile and looks around. When the clapping dies away, Spider says, "Where do we go from here?"

Coach Pack says, "I have made up my mind about the two of you. One of you is going to start from now on. The other is going to be our 6th man. Next week, as you know, we're going to play the Sharks. I don't have to tell you how big this game is. You all know the Sharks are good. We beat them once, but the next game will be in their city on their court. We'll be far from home. The crowd will be against us. To win, we'll have to really pull together as a team. The last time we won both our games against the Sharks, we went on to play for the state championship. That was 22 years ago. Men, I don't mind telling you **I want this game**! If any of you don't want it just as badly, you don't belong on this team. That said, let's look at our problem. Spider, you get a big hand from all of us. Looking after that lost boy shows character. But you haven't been giving 100% to this team. Tyrone, you've been playing monster ball of late. You work hard. You leave it all on the floor. But telling these stories about Spider was bad—just bad. A thing like that can break a team apart."

"I thought I was doing something to help the team," says Tyrone.

"He said it won't happen again," Mack puts in. "Spider is ready to let it go. Doesn't that count for something?"

"Maybe," says Coach Pack, "but I'm still going to start Spider—if he's ready to give us what we need from him. Next week, I'm going to run practice from 3:00 to 5:00. I'm going to ask you all to come back after dinner and shoot free throws. Spider, you will have to tell me if you can put in that kind of time. It's only for a week. If you're ready for it, you're my man. Tyrone," he turns to the other boy, "I'm going to bring you off the bench as our 6th man. Now a good 6th man can be the most important guy on a team. He can be the **go to** guy at the end of a close game. You do a lot of things well, Tyrone. But there has always been a question mark hanging over 1 part of your game: can you be a team player? If the answer is no, you can never be great. As 6th man, you have a chance to show me this part of your game. As 6th man you have a chance—just a chance, mind you—to be great."

"I won't let you down, Coach."

"Tell it to the team," says Coach Pack.

9. The Has-Been

That night, Spider says, "Aunt. Uncle. I have something to tell you."

"What?" says his uncle.

Spider tells what happened at basketball practice that day. "This next week, I have to cut back my hours at the shop, just till we get through this next game."

"Oh," says his uncle, "what if you win this game?"

"Well, then we go on to—"

"Another game," says his uncle. "Then one more and one more. Believe me, Coach will tell you each game is bigger than the last. Every week he will cry about how much he counts on you. He knows every trick in the book, Spider. He made it to the state championship game one time as a young man. He's never been back. He'll drive you boys into the ground to get what he wants."

"So what?" Spider cries out. "Don't you think we all want what he wants? The whole team wants that medal. They won't get it without me. I can't let them down."

"There are times, Spider, when a man has to think of himself," his uncle says.

"Don't you think it would mean something to me?" cries Spider.

His uncle gets red in the face. "What will it mean? Your picture in the paper? You'll have a book you can open years later to show your kids. Look, you'll say, here I am shaking hands with so and so. Don't you get it? This is just high school. Where will you go from here? You think some college will give you money to play ball? Dream on. Out there in the big, cold world, no one knows your name. Out there, no one knows the Sharks from the Cougars. No one cares which of you win or lose. There are hot basketball players all over the country. There are 1,000 players ahead of you for every place open in college. Even if you play college ball, what then? The NBA? Give me a break. You're too short! Don't you get it? You might grow to 6'4" at most. In the big time, that's short—they'll eat you alive."

"But I'm good," Spider says.

"Who says? Your Coach! Of course, he will tell you anything he has to, anything that will make you play hard. Who else? Kids around school? That Venus? What do they know? We're not talking about next week or the week after, Tom. We're talking about your whole life here. There are a lot of years after high school—a lot of years!"

Tom's aunt gets up. "I'll let you guys talk this out," she says. But at the door, she turns to add: "You listen to your uncle, Tom. He's done his best to raise you right. All he wants is what is best for you. He knows about these things. He's been through them. You listen to him, Tom."

The door shuts. Tom's uncle starts right in again. "You think I'm being hard on you, Tom, but think about the other side. After high school, you can come into the business full time. Pretty soon you'll be making good money— enough to go out and get your own place. Start a family. Be a man. I look at you as my own kid, Spider. One day I will not be around anymore, and you will take over. Why do you think I am working so hard to build the business up? For you, Spider. I'm giving you a chance at real security. You act like it's nothing? Like it's nothing, what I'm giving you. No, they don't put your name in lights for this kind of work. No one comes around from the paper and takes your picture. You don't get to run around with stars, and you sure don't get rich. All you get is security, and a chance to hold your head high. Because everyone has a car, and every car breaks down. Am I getting through to you, Tom?"

"I don't know."

"You don't know! What is it that you don't know?"

"I don't know if you can see me, Uncle."

"What do you mean? Of course, I can see you. You're sitting right there across the table!"

"I mean really see me. I feel like you look right through me. You see yourself maybe. You see your own hopes or something. You've done a lot for me, Uncle. I know that—it means the world to me. But all my life I have been no one special. No one ever really looked at me. No one saw me. Now all of a sudden, there is something I can do really well, and it makes me feels good about myself. You say it's just a game, and it isn't worth anything. It's like you're saying I'm not worth anything. But I say anything a guy can do is worth something. Playing ball makes me feel good about myself. I just don't know why you want to take that away from me."

"Oh, Tom—I don't want to take anything away from you. You're worth so much more than you think. This game makes you put your worth too low! Let me show you something. Stay there. I'll be right back."

His uncle leaves the room for a minute and comes back with a big book. He opens it up. The book has stories and pictures cut from old newspapers. The paper is all yellow. The stories are about Tom's uncle—as a baseball player.

"Yes, Tom," says his uncle, "I, too, was a star in high school. You don't know that because I never talk about it anymore. But everyone said I was the best player to come out of these parts in 50 years. It went to my head. I left school early. I started to play class AA ball. My numbers were good. Every year the big boys said I was going to 'The Show'— the big time—soon. Back then the money was just starting to be good. Two of my friends were called up to The Show. They ended up rich. I waited for the same thing to happen to me. While I was waiting, I let my life pass me by. I could have done so much more, Tom. If only I had not thrown away so many years playing class AA ball in some little town. Hope was like a drug to me. The dream of fame and money was like a drug! I couldn't let it go. Then one day I was 31 years old, and they let me go. They said you're old, you're slow, your numbers are down. You're done. What was I supposed to do then? I didn't know anything. I didn't have any kind of job skill. I was just an old, slow has-been. But I pulled myself together, Tom. I went to work. All the other workers at this job were boys. Younger guys would order me around. But I put money away every chance I had. I did my best to pick up some real life skills. As soon as I could, I went into business for myself. You think it was easy building up The Body Shop? Think again! I look back now on all those years of playing ball—what do I have to show for them? A few old newspaper stories and these pictures that no one wants to look at. Most times, if I bring them out, people feel sorry for me. Poor old has-been, they say to themselves. High point of his whole life was a game in high school. I don't want that to happen to you, Tom. Now do you understand?"

"More than I did before, Uncle."

"Good. Then you'll go into Coach Pack tomorrow and let him know. Tell him if it comes down to a choice between his team or your life, you would pick your own real life."

"No."

"What?"

"I said no. I am not going to let my team down. I can't let myself down. Your story is your story, Uncle. I'm not thinking about the NBA, or the big money, or hanging out with stars. I've gotten through all that. It's just about me now, and what I can do. It's about coming through after you have given your word. Uncle Robert, the 11 guys on my team count on me—and Coach makes 12. If I let them down, I can't hold my head up."

"Tom, I don't think you get the point. Let me put it on the table. Either you leave the team, or you let go of this job. You can't have it both ways."

"I'm not going to leave the team, Uncle, and I'm not going to let my job go. You will have to fire me."

"Don't test me. I'll do it. I'm a man of my word. If I say I am going to do something, I do it. Don't think I won't fire you."

"Did you just fire me?" Spider asks.

"No—but I might. Don't think I won't. I just might."

"Let me know if you do," says Spider, and he gets up.

His aunt has just come into the room. "Where are you going?"

"I have to go see Little Bill. I won't see much of him this next week. I have to tell him why and let him know that I still care. Just like I still care about you, Aunt and Uncle, even if you think I am letting you down."

10. Body Not Found

The Cougars leave for the big game in a special bus. They get to the other city a little before 12:00. Coach Pack wants the team to practice on this floor and then take some time to rest and get ready.

The practice ends at 1:00. After they eat, they have some free time. "Don't go too far," says the coach. "I want you all back by 4:00."

"Where would we go?" laughs Tyrone.

"Maybe we can catch a movie," says Mack. "Shoot that newspaper to me, Spider."

But Spider does not hear him. A small heading on an inside page has caught his eye: **Body of Boy Still Not Found**. He reads the story with growing interest. Some weeks back, it seems there was a bad fire in this city. It started in a clothes shop.

The building burned to the ground. One little boy died in the fire—or so everyone thinks. The boy had come to the shop with his mom. When the fire started, he could not be found. Everyone else got out safe. But the boy must have died in the fire. His body, however, was not found later. The fire chief said there would not be much to find after a fire like that. But in time, he thought some bones and teeth would turn up. The news today was only that there was no news. No teeth and no bones had been found yet. The fire chief did not know what to make of it.

Spider puts down the newspaper. He is thinking about Little Bill. He remembers what Peary of Missing Persons said. Any family that loses a kid tells the police about it. They ask the cops to look for their kid. Why is no one looking for Bill? Suddenly Spider knows he has the answer.

What if the family doesn't think the kid is missing? What if they think he died? If it was the same boy, how did he get out of the shop? How did he get to another city over 100 miles away? How did he lose his memory?

Spider can't sit still. The newspaper gives the name of the shop that burned down. The yellow pages still have an ad for it. Spider finds out where it is and goes out to the street. Finding the right bus takes ten minutes. The trip to that part takes another 20. When he gets there, Spider finds an empty lot, of course. The building is gone. Signs tell him not to walk over that ground. He doesn't want to. There is nothing to see there anyway—just some burned sticks.

Spider stands there, trying to picture the building. A man comes out of a restaurant across the street and walks over to Spider.

"I was there, you know," says the man.

"What?" Spider turns to him.

"Yes. My sister was shopping in there. I came to pick her up—we almost were caught in the fire."

"What was it like?" Spider asks.

"I have never been so scared in my life," the man tells him. "People were screaming. You couldn't see a thing. The air was so hot, so black."

"Did you know the kid who died?"

"No. That was so sad. It was just one of those things. I don't hold it against the mom. You can't watch a kid every second. She was trying on clothes. There was no way she could know a fire was about to start. Once it started, there was no way to find the kid. People were running every which way, screaming their heads off. They had to pull her out. Then they had to hold her down. She wanted to go back in and look for him. But it was too late. She would only have died herself.

Spider looks past the man. He sees a truck stop and a parking lot. These would have been behind the building that is now gone. Then Spider sees a big truck in the parking lot. It's a truck that takes new cars from city to city.

Suddenly Spider remembers Bill's "bad dream." Only Bill said it wasn't a dream. He said he could remember lots of cars—new cars. All of them were moving, but not one of them had a driver. Spider now sees what Bill might have been remembering. At that moment, the truck driver comes out of the restaurant. He is wearing green.

A wave of excitement goes through Spider. "Was there a back door to this shop?" he wants to know. "Could someone have walked out that door to the parking lot over there?"

"Sure. I guess so," says the man. "Why?"

"I just had a thought," says Spider, and he takes off running.

Spider calls the cops from the first telephone he can find. He starts to tell the man who answers about the lost boy. Maybe he is too excited. The cop stops him in the middle of his story. "Yes. Yes. OK. We'll look into it," he says, and he hangs up.

He won't look into it. Maybe cops get calls like this all the time. But now Spider doesn't know what to do. Should he go to the fire house? Then he has a better idea. Newspapers are always looking for stories. This would sure be a story.

Spider doesn't try to use the telephone. He finds out where the newspaper office is and takes a bus right to the building. Inside he tells a woman what he wants. "Who should I talk to?" he asks.

She points to a man who is just walking out the door. "Try Tom over there. He was on the fire story, I think."

Tom. That's Spider's own real name. A good sign. Spider runs after the man. "Tom," he calls out, "may I talk to you? I have a story that might interest you."

"Make it fast," says the writer. "I'm on a break."

Spider tells him the whole story of Bill and the boy in the fire.

The writer is interested. "Oh!" he says. "If this turns out like you say, what a story! Front page! I was at that fire, you know— That boy's mom— I have never seen anyone cry so hard."

"Call her right now," says Spider.

"No. I can't do that yet," says Tom. "I can't get her hopes up before I look into it myself. If this turns out to be a different boy... It would just kill her. But you know what? Come up to my office. I still have pictures of that boy from the fire. Miles, I think his name was. You look at them and see what you think."

He takes Spider to the newsroom. He puts a small picture of a boy in front of him. The boy is about five years old. Spider only has to look once. "That's him."

"Are you sure?" The writer is excited.

"It's him, I tell you. He's living in a foster home in my town. Over there we're calling him Bill. Now will you call his parents?"

"I don't know. I still have to make sure. Where did you say you live?" When Tom hears the name of the city, he shakes his head. "That's over 100 miles. I can't get away that long today—"

"Then go to the police here," says Spider. "Go to Missing Persons. I'm sure they have Bill's picture. You can look at it and see for yourself."

"OK, good idea. You're on." The writer picks up the picture of Miles. "Let's go."

But Spider looks at his watch and shakes his head. "I can't. I have to be at a basketball game. I play for a high school team called the Cougars, and tonight—"

"I know the Cougars," says Tom. "I used to play for the Sharks many years ago. I'm going to that game tonight."

"Great! Will you look me up after the game and tell me what happened?" says Spider.

"No problem," says Tom.

11. The Big Game

At 7:00 the floor lights up. The doors are closed. The place is full—they could not pack in 1 more person if they tried. The crowd starts making noise as soon as the first introduction starts. As each name is called out, a guy runs out. Spider is shaking with excitement. He hears the words, "And now let's have a big hand for the COUGARS!" After that, the words die away in a storm of white noise. Of his own name, all he hears is "Spider," and out he goes.

The two teams face off and shake hands. Then the bench guys run to the side. The others stay on the floor and wait. The Sharks get the ball first. They run off ten points, just like that. Coach Pack calls time out. He talks to his team in a low, quiet voice. "Stay calm," he says. "You can take these guys." He sets up a play. The Cougars go out, and **they** run off ten points.

After that, the game turns into a real dog fight. First one team goes up. Then the other makes a run. The Cougars never get ahead by more than four points. Once, late in the game, they are down by five. After that, slowly they even the score.

Then suddenly the Sharks make a run. They score two points. Then they score two more, and then two more. In just 32 seconds, the Cougars find themselves six points behind. Coach Pack calls time.

"What's wrong with you guys?" His voice is still quiet, but he sounds mad. His face is red. "Are you scared? Did you come here to lose? You already beat this team once. Remember? Spider! Move your feet out there, man! Tyrone. Off the bench. You're going in—no, not for Spider. For Matthew. I'm going to play you and Spider at the same time. We need power out there."

Spider and Tyrone look at each other. Then the buzzer sounds, and they head back out. Tyrone says to Spider: "You and me. Let's blanket them."

The moment play starts, Tyrone is all over his man. Suddenly he has stolen the ball! Spider doesn't wait to see what will happen. He takes off on a break. Tyrone passes the ball way out ahead of him. Then it's a foot race between Spider and one of the Sharks. Spider wins, he scores, and he gets a free throw, too. That shot goes in, making it a three-point play. The Cougars are only down by three.

The Sharks try to slow down the game after that. They run 39 seconds off the clock, just holding the ball. But in the end their guard drives to the basket, and Spider blocks his shot. This time it is Tyrone who takes off on the break. He scores at the other end. Two more points! The Cougars are only down by one. Spider looks up at the clock. Ten seconds left in the game—and the Sharks have the ball.

They call time. Coach Pack gets his players into a circle. "Listen up, men. We need the ball back," he says. "Make them shoot free throws if you have to. But first go for the steal. If you steal the ball, fire it to Spider. He will take it up the floor, pass it back to Dan, and cut to the basket. The Sharks will run two players in to stop him. That will leave someone open on the outside. Dan, you pass it to whoever is open. That guy takes a shot right away. Got that?"

The Cougars all say, "Yes." Both teams run back out to the floor. One of the Sharks tries to throw the ball over Tyrone's head. Bad move. Tyrone jumps high and steals the ball. He puts it on the floor once and looks up the court. Spider is running. Tyrone himself could drive all the way to the basket and maybe score. But he runs the set play. He passes it up to Spider. Spider gets it back to Dan. Then he burns right past a Shark, going for the basket. But only one man follows him. The Sharks didn't fall for it. No one is open on the outside. Dan looks scared. Time is running down. He has no one to pass to. He will have to take the shot himself. He jumps. He shoots. But there is a Shark right in his face, and his shot is way off. It hits the top of the basket and goes back up. Spider goes up after it.

Then it happens. Time slows down for Spider, as it sometimes does. He sees that he can catch the ball. But he can't put it in the basket. The man guarding him will block it. He won't have time to land and go back up. Then he sees Tyrone standing a few feet away. Spider doesn't catch the ball. He just hits it with his open hand. The ball goes right to Tyrone. Tyrone puts up a jump shot. It falls through the basket just as the buzzer sounds.

The game is over. Tyrone won it.

The Cougars run off the floor, waving their hands high. They crowd around Coach Pack, who is laughing and trying to shake all their hands at once.

Spider is part of that group, but only for a second or two. Then he remembers that Tom from the newspaper will be looking for him. He had better get out where he can be seen. As he leaves the crowd, Venus goes past him. Her eyes are on Tyrone. Spider smiles and looks through the crowd of faces. Suddenly he see some faces that he knows: his aunt, his uncle, and Mark are coming his way. His aunt is wearing a big smile on her face. His uncle has his hand out.

Spider says, "Uncle Robert! What are you doing here?"

"I came to fire you!" his uncle cries out. Then he shakes Spider's hand. "Just kidding!"

Spider doesn't know what to say or think. He tries to tell his uncle how moved he feels. But at that moment he sees someone else and his mouth falls open. Bill is running toward him with open arms.

"How in the world did you get here!" Spider cries. "Did your foster parents—"

But Diana comes up just then. "He's with me," she smiles. "Bill called me and said he wanted to see this game. He talked me into going. I called your aunt and uncle. They called the social worker. She called the foster parents. They called your aunt and uncle. They called me, and here we all are. That Little Bill! He knows how to get things going for such a little guy!"

Spider says, "But I thought you never—"

"Go to basketball games? I don't. I wasn't going to. But I couldn't let Bill down, could I? You know something. This game was fun to watch."

"I'm happy to hear you say it." Spider puts his arm around Bill and pulls the little boy close. "I'm really happy that you're here, Bill. There is someone you should meet. He's in this crowd somewhere. We have to look around for him. He's—"

Spider stops talking. Even without looking down, he can tell that something has happened to the little boy. When he does look down, he sees that Bill's mouth is hanging open. His eyes are as big as dinner dishes.

Diana is scared. "What's wrong, Bill?"

Spider follows the line from Bill's eyes to the crowd. He sees Tom from the newspaper first of all. Then he sees a woman next to Tom—

someone Spider has never seen before. Then he sees the man next to the woman. The man and woman are walking toward Bill, hand in hand, but they look like they are about to fall over. Both have faces as white as snow. The woman looks like she's trying to talk, but no words are coming out. The man looks like winter turning into summer. Then at last the woman finds her voice. "Miles!" she screams.

At that sound, Bill is suddenly gone. There is no Bill and never has been. The little boy standing next to Spider is Miles. He is no longer lost. "Mom," he cries. "Oh, Dad." He runs to them.

"We thought—" The woman has a hard time getting the words out. "We thought you had died." She looks at Spider over her little boy's head. "I wanted to die myself." Her voice breaks. After a minute, she goes on. "Tom told me what you have done. But no one can ever really tell you what you have done for us. You have given me my life back." Then she and her husband are both crying. The little boy is crying, too. Spider can feel his own eyes starting to water. He looks at Diana and sees that she is close to crying, too.

"It was nothing," he says. But that doesn't seem right. It **was** something after all.

"Mom," Little Bill cries. "Oh, Dad." He runs to them.

12. The Whole Story

Miles gets his memory back, but not all at once. It's a long time before Spider knows the whole story. In the end, he does find out this much. On the day of the fire, Miles was in the shop with his mom and his aunt. They were trying on clothes. He lost interest as little boys will. He went looking around for something to play with in the store and found the back door open. Outside, he saw a truck with new cars on it. He thought it might be fun to play at driving one of the cars. He thought he would get back long before his mom was done.

But while he was in the car, the truck started to move. He tried to leave, but the door would not open. Maybe he was too scared to work it right. Anyway, the truck was soon on the freeway. The boy screamed for help, but no one could hear him. After a long while, he went to sleep.

How he hit his head, no one knows to this day. He might have fallen when the truck made a sudden stop. Miles only remembers that he was in the truck, and night was falling. His head hurt. He didn't know who or where he was.

The truck stopped. This time he got the door open. He started to leave, but his foot caught on something and down he went. The truck driver saw him just then picking himself up off the ground. He must have thought Miles was some little kid from the neighborhood. He sure didn't want kids playing around on his truck. If one of them got hurt, he could be in trouble. So he did his best to drive the boy away. He waved his hands and screamed at him. But Miles did not understand. He was scared, and so he started to run. He didn't stop till he found a place to hide. That place happened to be the park.

That year Spider and Tyrone gave Coach Pack his first championship ring. Tyrone went on to play college ball for one of the big schools. He even made it into the NBA for a year. Spider got money to play for a small college in the south. He never was famous, and he never did play in the NBA. But that was all right with him. By then Spider had learned what he really wanted to do with his life—which was to help people. As it turned out, he was good at it. He was even better at helping people than he was at basketball. He had a skill that is hard to find in this world—he could feel what other people were feeling.

Spider never lost his love of basketball. In the end, he found a way to put his two skills together. When Spider was 25, Coach Pack died. He was asked to be the new coach at JFK High. Spider was happy to take the job—and he is still there today. Most years his team wins more than it loses. Some years it loses more than it wins. But guys who play for Coach Spider always seem to do all right in life.